Usborne

Little First Stickers

Cats and Kittens

Illustrated by Nicole Standard

You can find all the stickers at the back of the book.

Words by Caroline Young
Designed by Maddison Warnes

Playtime

Coco has had eight kittens, so she's a very busy mother! Add stickers to show where they all are, and some toys for them to play with.

Coco carries her kittens around very gently, like this. It doesn't hurt them at all.

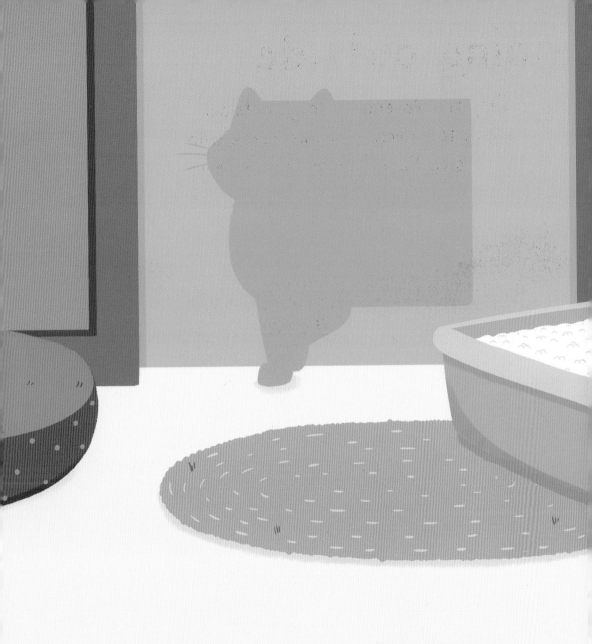

The kittens are growing fast.
They need plenty of food
and water nearby.

Going outside

When they are old enough to go outside, kittens love to explore. Fill this scene with stickers to give them lots to see and enjoy.

Kittens often chase anything that moves, like these fluttering butterflies.

Coco keeps a watchful
eye on her kittens
all the time.

At the vet

Katie and her dad are taking their cat, Millie, to the vet because Millie's not well. Can you add stickers to show what happens?

Don't worry. The vet will help her.

Vets do lots of different things to help animals stay well.
Use the stickers to show some of them here.

Cats are weighed at
the vet, to check they
are healthy.

This cat needs an X-ray to
see if it has a broken bone.

Some cats need
special food from
the vet.

After an operation, a cat needs to heal.
The vet might give it a cone to stop it
from licking or scratching the wound.

Lots of cats

Did you know that there are lots of different kinds of cats? Match the stickers to the shapes on these pages to see some of them.

Ginger

Tuxedo

Black

Tabby

Tortoiseshell

Ragdoll cats are born white
and get their markings later.

Bengal cats
have spots.

Persian cats
have long,
fluffy coats.

LaPerm cats
have curly fur.

Russian Blue cats are not really blue.
They all have green eyes though.

On the farm

Both the big cats on this farm have had kittens.
They all play together in the barn and snuggle up there
at night. Add stickers to complete this busy scene.

When they are grown up,
the kittens will probably
catch mice on the farm.

Being a mother can be tiring! Can you add two snoozing mother cats?

These kittens have plenty of playmates. Stick on some more.

Cat café

This café is special, because you can come here to spend time with cats, if you want to. It's the end of a busy day, so all the cats are relaxing.

Many people find being around cats makes them feel calmer.

The café has many toys for the cats to play with. Stick on some more.

Unusual cats

The cats on this page are a little unusual, so you might not have seen them before. Match the stickers to the shapes to find out more.

The largest kind of pet cat is a Maine Coon.

The smallest pet cat is a Singapura.

Peterbald cats have webbed feet.

Khao Manee cats can have one gold and one blue eye.

Turkish Van cats love water.

Siamese cats
have blue eyes.

Sphynx cats
have no fur.

American Curl cats
have curled-back ears.

Munchkin cats
have short legs.

Lykoi cats are also called
Wolf cats, as they look a
little like small wolves.

Pixie-bob cats
have tiny tails
like rabbits.

Showtime!

There are some amazing cats at the show today.
Their owners are excited, wondering who will win.

Which cat do
you think should
win each prize?

Friendliest Face

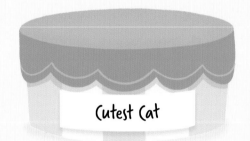

Cutest Cat

Longest Tail

Best in Show

Fluffiest Fur

Give each winner a
ribbon, then give the cup
to the Best in Show.

Catflap

Brush

Kittens

Toys

Scratching post

Going outside pages 4-5

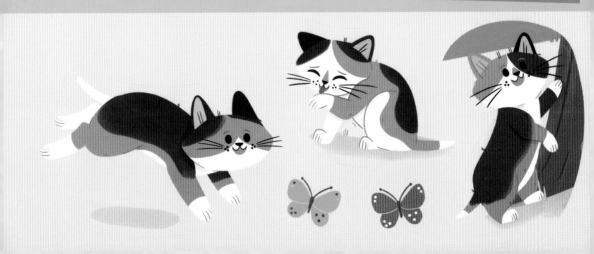

At the vet

Cat carrier

Millie keeps sneezing all the time.

This medicine will help Millie feel better very soon.

Vet

X-ray

Special food

Cat on weighing scales

Lots of cats pages 8-9

Tabby

Persian

Bengal

Tuxedo

LaPerm

Tortoiseshell

Ginger

Ragdoll

Russian Blue

Black

On the farm

Mice

Unusual cats pages 14-15

Singapura

Maine Coon

Munchkin

Peterbald

Pixie-bob

Turkish Van

Khao Manee

Sphynx

Siamese

Lykoi

American Curl

Showtime! page 16